My school community

Bobbie Kalman

 Crabtree Publishing Company

www.crabtreebooks.com

Created by Bobbie Kalman

Author and Editor-in-Chief
Bobbie Kaiman

Educational consultants
Reagan Miller
Joan King
Elaine Hurst

Editors
Joan King
Reagan Miller
Kathy Middleton

Proofreader
Crystal Sikkens

Design
Bobbie Kalman
Katherine Berti

Photo research
Bobbie Kalman

Production coordinator
Katherine Berti

Prepress technician
Katherine Berti

Photographs
iStockphoto: p. 1, 6, 7, 9, 14, 20 (right),
    23 (top right), 24 (top left)
All other photographs by Shutterstock

Library and Archives Canada Cataloguing in Publication

Kalman, Bobbie, 1947-
    My school community / Bobbie Kalman.

(My world)
Includes index.
ISBN 978-0-7787-9442-4 (bound).--ISBN 978-0-7787-9486-8 (pbk.)

    1. Schools--Juvenile literature. 2. School environment--Juvenile
literature. I. Title. II. Series: My world (St. Catharines, Ont.)

LB1513.K35 2010   j372   C2009-906102-3

Library of Congress Cataloging-in-Publication Data

Kalman, Bobbie.
My school community / Bobbie Kalman.
    p. cm.
Includes index.
ISBN 978-0-7787-9486-8 (pbk. : alk. paper) -- ISBN 978-0-7787-9442-4
(reinforced library binding : alk. paper)
1. Schools--Juvenile literature. 2. Classrooms--Juvenile literature.
I. Title.

LB1513.K36 2010
371--dc22
                                                    2009041221

Crabtree Publishing Company

www.crabtreebooks.com   1-800-387-7650

Printed in China/122009/CT20091009

Published in Canada
Crabtree Publishing
616 Welland Ave.
St. Catharines, Ontario
L2M 5V6

Published in the United States
Crabtree Publishing
PMB 59051
350 Fifth Avenue, 59th Floor
New York, New York 10118

Published in the United Kingdom
Crabtree Publishing
Maritime House
Basin Road North, Hove
BN41 1WR

Published in Australia
Crabtree Publishing
386 Mt. Alexander Rd.
Ascot Vale (Melbourne)
VIC 3032

What is in this book?

My school is a community

A **community** is a group of people.
A community is also a place where
people work together and share things.
People in a community help one another.

My school is a community.

People at my school work together.

We help one another learn.

Our classroom

Our school community is in a **building**.

The school building has many classrooms.

Children of the same age are in a **grade**.

We learn together in the same classroom.

Our teacher teaches us.

Sharing with others

People in a community share things.
At school, we share classrooms, books,
paper, paint, and computers.
We share sports equipment.

We share our teachers, too.

We could not learn without them.

Our teachers teach us how to read and write.

They make learning fun!

Traveling to school

People in communities **travel**.

To travel is to go from place to place.

I travel to school in a school bus.

Some of my friends walk or ride their bikes to school.

Most of my friends
take the bus to school.

A good education

School is a community for **education**.

I learn **information** and **skills** at school.

Getting a good education is the best thing I can do for myself.

Getting an education is also a lot of fun.

I love learning math. It is my favorite **subject**. What is your favorite subject?

In science, I learn information about animals. I also learn skills, like how to use a **microscope**.

microscope

When I grow up, I want to be a writer. At school, I am learning how to write and how to use the computer.

Jobs at school

My teacher has a good education.

You need a good education to be a teacher.

My teacher earns money for doing his job.

Our job is to learn as much as we can!

Our **librarian** lends books to teachers and students.
She also helps us find information in books and on the computer.

Our **principal** runs the school. She makes sure that everyone follows the rules.

School rules

Communities have **laws**, or rules.
We have rules at school, too.
We follow rules to help
ourselves and others.

Rules
- Be kind and helpful to others.
- Show respect to teachers and students.
- Share books and other school supplies.
- Keep your area neat and clean.
- Put your hand up to answer questions.
- Act safely with yourself and others.
- Do your best every day.

I show respect
to my teacher.

17

Different cultures

Culture is how people live.
History, music, food, religion,
and clothing are parts of culture.
How people celebrate
is also part of culture.
Children from many
cultures go to my school.
We learn about one
another's cultures.

I play Polish music
on my accordion.

I eat Japanese
food with
chopsticks.

I am a Muslim.
I always cover
my head.

We are wearing
shirts that show
our African culture.

19

Fun at school

Communities are places to have fun.

My school community is a fun place!

We paint, play music, and dance.

We play sports, too.

At school, we learn to play **musical instruments**, such as trumpets and tambourines.

tambourine

trumpet

We play soccer and other sports.

We talk, laugh, and have fun with our friends.

Keeping healthy

Communities try to keep people healthy. It is hard to keep healthy at school because many children sit close together. These are some things we can do to help keep healthy.

We can wash our hands with soap many times a day. While we wash, we sing the "Happy Birthday" song.

We can stay at home when we feel sick.

We can sneeze into our arms and not into our hands.

If we feel sick at school, we can visit the school nurse.

Words to know and Index

classroom
pages 6–7, 8

cultures
pages 18–19

education
pages 12–13, 14

fun
pages 12, 20–21

jobs
pages 14–15

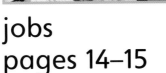

rules
pages 15, 16–17

sharing
pages 4, 8–9, 16

keeping healthy
pages 22–23

travel
pages 10–11